*2 Chapbooks / One Multidimensional Memoir**

hänen äänsä : a HYBRID MEMOIR

Her
Voice / Voice
Over

a memoir breakout in 7 movies

Praise for **Voice / Over**

This screenplay + memoir + photo collage album is as rich and complex as a hybrid memoir gets. Weaving together politics, voting rights and classic filmography, *Voice/ Over* takes readers on an unforgettable multiracial, multigenerational adventure.

—**Susan Kiyo Ito**, author of *I Would Meet You Anywhere: A Memoir*, National Book Critics Circle Award finalist

*Both books are available at texasreviewpress.org

Voice/Over is a collage of images, form, politics, family and cultural history that journeys through 7 films to show voting as an act of resistance. From the Nordic family as James Bond Characters to Mummi's battle with cancer, the family of migrants in a small town are shot against a political backdrop of Watergate and narrated through twin voices of Faith as a babyface, 9-year-old, brown child in an all white family and sometimes [an] invisible college student, who both keep taking us back to this one voting day where Mummi casts her vote to save the free world.

—**Tara Dorabji,** author of *Call Her Freedom,*
winner of the Like Us First Novel Prize
from Simon & Schuster

What does it mean to seek home, despite loss and violent erasure? Intricate and epic, devastating and hilarious, Faith Adiele's remarkable quest is the story of every global diaspora.

—**Tracy K. Smith,** U.S. Poet Laureate and Pulitzer-prize-winning
author of *Life on Mars*

Part history lesson . . . part love letter . . . utterly captivating. A feast for the eyes, the mind, and the heart.

—**Natalie Baszile,** Author of *Queen Sugar,* now an acclaimed television
series from producers Ava duVernay & Oprah Winfrey

A comic's timing, a novelist's keen observations about human idiosyncrasies, and an anthropologist's sensitivity to issues of race and culture.

—***Publishers Weekly,*** starred review of *Meeting Faith*

Adiele's account of her life is witty, mutinous, unflinchingly self-aware. An assured storyteller . . . her closely observed details startle with their exactness.

—**Rosemarie Robotham,** *Black Issues Book Review*

An extraordinary book—part memoir . . . part spiritual journey and completely generous.

—***Elliot Bay Booknotes***

Voice /over

a memoir breakout in 7 movies

Faith Adiele

★trp

The University Press of SHSU
Huntsville, Texas 77341
texasreviewpress.org

Library of Congress Control Number: 2024935120

Voice/Over: a memoir breakout in 7 movies / Faith Adiele
ISBN: 9781680033618 (paperback)
Cover & book design: PJ Carlisle
Collages: Faith Adiele
Front cover photo: Myke Simon @unsplash.com
Title font: Afronaut by Mateusz Machalski, Poland
FIRST EDITION
Printed and bound in the United States of America

TRP: The University Press of SHSU
Huntsville, Texas 77341
texasreviewpress.org

For Mom
and everyone who sacrificed for voting rights
and sacrifices still

Contents

The Family

(in Order of Appearance)

(VOICE/OVER): According to the Screenwriter's Bible, Voice/Over (V.O.) notes a voice coming from outside the scene. It can be the character narrating the story. It can be the character's internal thoughts. It can be the liminal space en route to a flashback or whispers from another world (see *Her Voice/Hänen Ääensä*).

According to the Screenwriter's Bible, both spoken dialog and Voice/Over are centered on the page, one inch from the left margin. But let's be honest, my people speak from the margins. And we don't have much use for Bibles. Having been raised Left among the Christian Right, I'm itching to take back the Right.

See me here, occupying the right-hand margin, sometimes voice, sometimes character in scene, e.g. 9-Yr-Old Faith (VOICE/OVER).

9-YR-OLD FAITH: The only Brown person ("Black-and-white-make-brown") in the house. Apprentice bookworm committed to righting wrongs.

Likes to say things like: "No fair!" Suffers from Being the Only Black Girl in School-ism.

MUMMI LEMPI (ALMOST 60): Youngest daughter of Finnish immigrants, newly white mother of two (mummi is Finnish for grandmother). Soft-spoken amateur-artist, -chef, -baker, proto-domestic goddess, and a power example to her granddaughter, Faith.

Likes to say things like: "Two wrongs don't make a right." Suffers from Long-Suffering.

MORFAR GIB (ALSO ALMOST 60): Son of a Swedish immigrant, one of twelve kids, also newly white. Opinionated patriarch (morfar is Swedish for maternal grandfather), union organizer, and construction foreman at the Hanford Nuclear Reservation.

Likes to say things like: "Prove it! Just because it's in this Goddamn Right Wing Newspaper or on television doesn't mean it's true." Suffers from Television News-induced Apoplexy and Tall Tale-ism.

MOM (HOLLY) (NOT YET EVEN 30): White American woman. Fierce single mother. Junior high school teacher. Dedicated bookworm and political junkie.

Likes to say things like: "Pfft, typical male behavior." Suffers from Not Giving a Damn-ism.

UNCLE MICHAEL-VÄINÖ (EARLY 20-SOMETHING): Single white American male. Mom's younger brother. Dashing, hard-partying uncle who rarely notices the rest of us. Sleeps late, still lives with his parents, keeps back-issues of *Playboy* magazines in empty beer boxes in his closet. Unskilled worker at manufacturing plants.

Likes to say things like: "Oh, you think you're too good?" Suffers from a different kind of Not Giving a Damn-ism.

TÄTI RAUHA (WON'T TELL): Oldest daughter of Finnish immigrants, first American, first to speak English. (Täti is Finnish for elderly auntie, which is something to keep in mind when addressing not-so-elderly aunties).

Likes to say things like, "It'll be a fine day when a young person can tell an older person anything!" Suffers from first American/oldest immigrant child-ism.

COLLEGE-AGE FAITH: Wide-eyed, bushy-haired, first-gen Ivy Leaguer. Cinephile and New Wave fan still committed to righting wrongs.

Likes to say things like: "Sunday is the new Friday (at the club)!" and "My final paper will resolve my identity issues!" Suffers from Not Knowing How to Resolve Her Identity-ism.

1 Hr. Till
the Polls Close

Election Day 1972
Rural Washington State
Pacific Northwest

1 — INT. FARMHOUSE KITCHEN — NIGHT

A cheery kitchen with cabinets painted an array of sherbet colors: tangerine, strawberry, blueberry, pistachio. The canary yellow table is set for dinner. Through the curtained windows, we see that it is dark outside. A brown child in Sears' Toughskins with X's on the back pockets stands close to an older white woman in a floral housedress.

> **9-YR-OLD FAITH (VOICE/OVER)**
> Mummi Lempi waits at the oven door holding her wind-up timer. I am there at her side, nose out, sniffing, snooping. She has Election Days marked on the kitchen calendar with a red star (the significance of this color choice will be revealed later). On Red Star days, chances are she'll toss a hodgepodge stew onto the Formica table, impatient to get to the real meat of the night—voting!

She yanks a pie (something quickish, like
lemon meringue) from beneath the broiler,
and I pinch my nose in protest against the
treacly stench of burnt sugar.

Everyone knows that her cookies (fourteen
Joulu varieties, ice box, bar, pan, roll,
drop, gun), breads (limppu, banana,
pulla, zucchini, nissua), and pies (Yakima
Valley apple, strawberry-rhubarb, Yakima
Valley peach, Oregon huckleberry, lemon
meringue, Oregon blueberry, chocolate
cream, Washington marionberry, banana
cream, Yakima Valley cherry) can make
a grown man weep.

9-YR-OLD FAITH
Meringue's icky!

MUMMI LEMPI
(in a lilting Finnish accent)
But fast! Now go be USE-ful.

Faith scurries into the next room where the sounds of excited voices
are heard.

2 — INT. LIVING ROOM — NIGHT

A lived-in room with a large picture window and dark neutral décor.
All the furnishing are Mid-century Modern except for an overstuffed
reclining chair positioned directly across from the console TV. An
older white man in dark gray work clothes and oilskin cap leans
forward in the recliner. A young white woman in a cotton shift dress

and a young white man in pressed designer jeans perch on the frieze divan, waving their hands. Once inside, young Faith pauses to take in all the ruckus.

> **9-YR-OLD FAITH (VOICE/OVER)**
> Morfar Gib, Mom, and Uncle Michael-Väinö are buzzing about how the polls are going Back East, three hours ahead of us. Morfar Gib tips back his cap and scratches his bald spot, the stag logo galloping in place on the hat's crown. It's not looking good. He grimaces. The McGovern-Shriver ticket needed to counter all the good press That Idiot Nixon got for opening up Red China in a week. Apparently it was closed for twenty years, which seems like a long time to be out of business.

> **MORFAR GIB**
> The week that changed the world. My ass!

As Morfar Gib (Mom's father) scoffs, Mom—long brown hair caught back in a stretchy headband—jabs a manicured finger at him and her brother, Uncle Michael-Väinö.

> **MOM**
> Well, yes, but *finally* some intelligent foreign policy.

> **9-YR-OLD FAITH (VOICE/OVER)**
> They all take deep breaths and start talking about something called "détente."

I look the word up in my red American Heritage pocket dictionary with the shiny gold embossing. Unlike everybody else in town, we don't hate The Communists, so we didn't have to "relax" in the first place. We just wish that it was a Democratic president tromping around the Great Wall with a crowd, a Democratic president using chopsticks at a banquet dinner, a Democratic president watching a ballet about women revolutionaries, a Democratic president who put "SALT" on this Cold War business with the Soviets. Mom starts waving her hands.

MOM

You know Nixon can't be trusted!

9-YR-OLD FAITH (VOICE/OVER).

Our Candidate wasn't her first choice. There were actually two women vying for the Democratic nomination this year! Congresswoman Shirley Chisholm, the first Black woman elected to Congress and the first Afro-American to run for a major party's presidential nomination, and Representative Patsy Mink, the first Asian American to run for the Democratic presidential nomination. I suspect Morfar Gib has loved George McGovern from the start. He's gonna end Vietnam and implement a minimum income. (Imagine!)

Plus, his running mate is a Kennedy. Sure,
they may be American royalty, but they're
Good Guys, on the side of
the Common Man.

We were worried for a while, when George
Wallace swept the south, pretending like he
wasn't the same governor who had Black
Civil Rights activists beaten in Alabama,
but then six months ago he got paralyzed
in an attempted assassination. We're for
gun control, so our feelings about this are
complicated.

I launch myself onto Morfar Gib, my nose
to his chest: sweat, wintergreen Skoal, Old
Spice aftershave, hoppy beer.

9-YR-OLD FAITH
(announcing to the room)
Mummi Lempi says dinner's on the table. Hurry!

9-YR-OLD FAITH (VOICE/OVER)
Politics momentarily forgotten, Morfar
Gib grins and flips me effortlessly over his
broad shoulder. As he stands up, I skim
down his back, headfirst, squealing. At
the last minute, he grabs my knees and
dangles me upside down over the carpet.
My stomach floats, like on a roller coaster
or playground swing.

MORFAR GIB
(teasing)
What's your hurry?

9-YR-OLD FAITH
(burping syllables)
E-lec-tion-day!

9-YR-OLD FAITH (VOICE/OVER)
Uncle Michael-Väinö, watching the two
of us with a face like his stomach hurts (or
is it just the cleft-palate scar tugging at his
mustache hairs?), snatches up his beer and
heads for the kitchen. He's too far away,
but I know his five-o'clock shadow and
tight Pink Floyd t-shirt smell of BRUT
33, a fragrance like the alfalfa pasture out
back had a baby with Mummi Lempi's
homemade gingersnaps and Mom's
Earl Grey tea.

MOM
(hissing at her brother as he passes)
Forchrissake, she's a *child*. It's not her fault
Morfar grandfathers better than he fathered.
Growthehellup!

3 — INT. BRIGHT FARM KITCHEN

Everyone is now seated around the Formica table.

9-YR-OLD FAITH (VOICE/OVER)
Mummi Lempi passes plates of stew,

                                          while Morfar Gib, driven mad by
                                          President Nixon, starts
                                          pounding the table.

MORFAR GIB
(shouting)
Any damn fool can see we're still bombing—!

MUMMI LEMPI
(pleading)
Gib, you vill give YOUR-self AH-poplexy.

9-YR-OLD FAITH (VOICE/OVER)
                                          She sees me, arms crossed, hands
                                          buried into my armpits,
                                          eying my plate warily.

MUMMI LEMPI
(whispers)
PO-tato.

9-YR-OLD FAITH
(squinting at her plate)
It better not be rutabaga.

MUMMI LEMPI
(curls her beauty-queen lips into a smile)
It is not.

MORFAR GIB
(red-faced)
Vietnamization, my ass!

9-YR-OLD FAITH
(squinting some more)
It better not be turnip.

MUMMI LEMPI
*(ever patient, shakes her head, pincurls
bobbing)*
I vould not do that.

9-YR-OLD FAITH
You did before!

MOM
(wryly)
And we're still paying the price.

9-YR-OLD FAITH
(still grousing)
It better not be parsnips.

9-YR-OLD FAITH (VOICE/OVER)
Impressed by my commitment to
resisting root vegetables, Morfar Gib
pats his belly and leans over my plate.
His gray workshirt protrudes over the
kind of large, ornate belt buckle favored
by cowboys.

MORFAR GIB
(chuckling)
Hey, you can give me anything you don't like.
Er, that meat in your way?

UNCLE MICHAEL-VÄINÖ
Yeah, lemme help you with Bambi there.

9-YR-OLD FAITH (VOICE/OVER)
I yip with indignation as Uncle
Michael-Väinö spears one of my meats
with his fork, but then he winks, and
I'm momentarily dazzled by this
rare attention. His Puka shell choker
gleams white against his red neck like
a moviestar smile. Like David Cassidy
from The Partridge Family singing
"I Think I Love You."
Maybe I think he loves me.

Our family is obsessed. Uncle Michael-
Väinö is obsessed with Racing Motocross.
And with doing Things He Shouldn't
Be Doing.I'm obsessed with fairness and
fairytales—Russian Red, Finnish White,
American Black. I'm obsessed with The
Jackson Five and The Brady Bunch. With
paper dolls and dollhouse miniatures. With
telling the truth and doing the right thing.
Mummi Lempi and her sister Rauha are
obsessed with Female Suffrage. Mom and
Morfar Gib are obsessed with Politics and
the Right Wing Assholes surrounding us.

TITLE CARD DISSOLVES to scene:

4 — EXT. FARMHOUSE IN FINLAND — DAY

A snowy scene, 1918. The siding of another, darker farmhouse serves as backdrop to four young housemaids in long white cotton pinafores that flap in the icy wind. Each shoulders a rifle with bayonet. As the VOICE OVER continues, a fifth woman, in cap and trousers, enters left, mounted upon a shaggy white pony. The Finnish women, members of the Red Guard, stare down the camera.

9-YR-OLD FAITH (VOICE/OVER)

In 1906, seven years before Mummi was born and eleven years before the Grand Duchy of Finland even became independent from Russia, Finland became the second country in the world to guarantee women the right to vote. The following year, 19 women were elected to Parliament, taking ten percent of the seats! That's 14 years before America, the so-called Leader of the Free World, gave women, well, *white* women, the vote. Though 17 years after (white) women won the vote for the first time here in the Washington Territories. But they lost it four years later, which is something that can happen apparently.

In 1915, two years after Mummi Lempi's birth and two years before Finland's official birth as a nation (the Bolshevik Revolution distracting Russia long enough for Finland to make a bid for independence), two more births occur: 1) modern-day cinema is supposedly born with 2) the release/birth of *Birth of a Nation*.

Enter young Mummi Lempi and Täti Rauha, who stand beside the
Finnish women, posing arm-in-arm in full-length fox coats and jaunty
cloche hats. They beam at the camera, dazzling as 1930s movie stars.
Before them their older (but not yet 60-Yr-Old) selves also enter. In
their perms, wool dresses, shiny stockings, and pearls, they appear
to sit on a snowdrift. Everyone gazes adoringly at 6-Yr-Old Faith,
sparkling in white dress, white ankle socks, and patent-leather Mary
Janes. Hair pulled into a sleek bun, young Holly holds her daughter
and whispers into her ear. Interrupted mid-play, Faith clutches a doll
to her chest and glares at the unseen cameraman.

9-YR-OLD FAITH (VOICE/OVER)
Mummi Lempi and I are a movie plot.
Birthed exactly five days and 50 years
apart. When each of us is four years old,
our fathers declare independence. Her
father doesn't want to be Russian anymore;
he wants to be Finnish. My father doesn't
want to be Nigerian, anymore than he
wanted to be British; he wants to be
Biafran. They are obsessed. And then they
are at war, but still optimistic. Finnish
Workers (The Reds!) pal up with the
Bolsheviks. Neither want to be ruled by
rich Russian Tsars with their fancy cakes
and jeweled palaces. It's like a fairy tale,
"Snow-White and Rose-Red." But the
Finnish Reds go to war with the Finnish
Whites, who want to keep things the way
they are, as whites tend to do.

Everyone behaves badly. While their
mother bathes at the public sauna,

Mummi Lempi and her sister Rauha and
brother Väinö (Uncle Michael-Väinö's
namesake) sit rapt through Workers'
Theater and Agitprop productions. When
the heroic Russian proletariat works the
underground printing presses in service of
the Glorious Revolution, they clutch tiny
hands to tiny hearts.
Hurrah!

Even better, the Red Guard includes 2,000
women, suffragettes-turned-soldiers, in all-
female units, just like Revolutionary China.
Huzzah! Speaking of propaganda—

5 — INT. DARKENED HARVARD CLASSROOM

Auditorium-style seating, movie projector running, 1980s. College-
Age Faith in a pink, knock-off, Oxford shirt pushes through the
leather-padded wooden doors into the classroom and sits on a
glistening wooden pew in the back row. On the screen at the front of
the room, we see grainy B&W footage and jerky sped-up movements
of *Birth of a Nation*. After a pause, Faith turns to look at the camera.

COLLEGE-AGE FAITH
(quiet but refusing to stage whisper)
Mom can protect me from the right-wing politics
and racism at my crap high school in rural
Washington state, but not from the so-called
best university in America, where in film class
after film class we're told that *Birth of a Nation*
is a Cinematic Masterpiece. That cinema shapes

reality, cinema can win hearts and minds, but also, Geez, chill out, it's only a movie.

As students in the surrounding rows attempt to shush her, she turns her back on them and continues to speak.

COLLEGE-AGE FAITH (CONT'D)
I prepare to be educated.

What I get are three interminable hours of Antebellum melodrama. Three hours of Civil War battles. Three hours of Reconstruction, where white actors in Blackface behave like beasts, lusting after white women, drinking whiskey, and eating fried chicken in Congress while passing laws encouraging interracial marriage so that there can be more children like me subjected to shit like this:

D. W. GRIFFITH'S

MARVELOUS PHOTOGRAPHIC SPECTACLE IN TWELVE REELS

The Clansman

————*or*————

"The Birth of a Nation"

Produced by D. W. GRIFFITH, the World's Foremost Producer

From the Novel by Thomas Dixon, Jr.

Cost
$500,000

Cast
18,000
People

3,000
Horses

It Took
Eight
Months to
Complete

Romance and Comedy Midst Historic
Scenes

Decisive Battles of the Civil War!
Sherman's March to the Sea!
The Burning of Atlanta!
Lee's Surrender at Appomattox!
What It Cost Mothers, Wives and Sisters!
The Assassination of President Lincoln!
The Rise of the Ku Klux Klan!
The Coming of the Prince of Peace!

Unique Theatre   Santa Cruz

5 **DAYS** Commencing
Wednesday September 8

Matinees Thursday, Saturday, Sunday   Prices 25c, 50c, 75c
Evenings 8:00, Matinees 2:00

The Clansman, aka, *The Birth of a Nation* movie poster

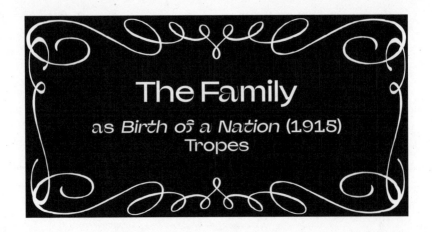

The Family
as *Birth of a Nation* (1915) Tropes

TITLE CARD DISSOLVES back to scene::

COLLEGE-AGE FAITH (CONT'D)
(reads the screen, full voice now)
The Family as *Birth of a Nation* Tropes—

Birth of a Nation on the classroom screen as Faith rises and strolls toward the front of the auditorium, speaking over her shoulder to the camera that follows her as she goes. Startled students turn to face her, a few taking notes, just in case this is on the test. *Birth of a Nation* continues to play on the screen. At the front, the professor hesitates then hands over his wooden pointer. Note: This is clearly a fantasy.

COLLEGE-AGE FAITH (CONT'D)
(expounds, mock-professor-style)
<u>ALL WHITE WOMEN</u>: (Mom? Mummi Lempi? Täti Rauha?) Portrayed by Lillian Gish, the character is the daughter of an abolitionist family who sees the error of her ways and marries a Confederate-soldier-turned-Klansman. Later she plays an abused white girl/half of cinema's

first interracial couple in *Broken Blossoms* (or *The Yellow Man and the Girl*). Conveniently, she dies before consummating her relationship with a white actor in Yellowface spouting Confucius. Suffers from professional suffering.

ALL MULLATTOS: (Me?) Silas Lynch, one of cinema's first mixed-race characters, is a psychopathic mulatto modeled on South Carolina's first Black lieutenant governor and the Haitian-American lawyer who served as the second. Portrayed by a white actor in Blackface, he drinks, he leers, he attempts rape. Suffers from Miscegenation Blues.

THE TRIUMPHANT MOVIE ENDING: One of the heroes establishes the Ku Klux Klan, riders and horses both draped in glorious glowing white, to make America great again. Northern and Southern whites unite against Blacks, their common enemy. On Election Day armed Klansmen stand outside homes, preventing Blacks from voting.

THE TRIUMPHANT REAL-LIFE ENDING: Despite Black protests, *Birth of a Nation* plays to packed movie houses with merchandise tie-ins. Americans rush to buy up KKK doodads and aprons. Ushers dress in white Klan robes and audiences organize Klan-themed balls. No one is canceled. The real Klan is revived just in time for the big Red Summer.

6 — EXT. STREET PROTESTS — NIGHT / DAY

SPLIT SCREEN, in full color & action: Black women in '40s overcoats and heels (NAACP members) carry protest signs under a glowing, pink, movie-theater marquee—another revival/screening of *Birth of a Nation*, while across the split young Black men in '60s-style suit jackets kneel in the hot sun in front of a federal building with their Right to Vote signs. In the center of all this (as if transported from the earlier scene (snowy 1918 Finland) Mummi Lempi, Täti Rauha, and Mom (6-yr-old Faith in her lap) float through, sitting in mid air. Gradually the scene DISSOLVES into the grainy B&W news-style footage seen on TV in the '70s, SUPERIMPOSED over the '80s classroom movie screening of *Birth of a Nation*, where the projector is still running.

7 — INT. DARKENED HARVARD CLASSROOM (CONT)

College-age Faith (pissed off) yanks the screen, and it retracts into a roll near the ceiling, quivering. *Birth of a Nation* and civil rights footage continue to play, SUPERIMPOSED atop the blackboard beneath. Suddenly, the images begin to melt as the projector (and footage) grinds to a stop. The classroom lights come up. The students, restless, stir in their seats.

How to Keep
Your Reds Straight
(1917-1921)

Faith, Mom, Täti Rauha, Mummi Lempi & Black women defend the free world.
You're welcome, America.

College-Age Faith reads the board and raps her pointer on the lectern for attention.

COLLEGE-AGE FAITH (CONT'D)
(writing on blackboard as she speaks, mock-lecture-style)

THE RED SCARE: The mass arrests and deportations of suspected communists and anarchists (Reds!), including Emma Goldman, from the USA.

RED DIAPER BABY: The child of parents who were members of or sympathetic to the American Communist Party. The child of any radical parent.

THE RED SUMMER: The violent race riots
(bloody!) started by whites against Blacks in
more than three dozen cities across the North
and South, most infamously, Tulsa, Oklahoma,
where for 24 hours, whites rampage Tulsa's Black
community, murdering men and women, looting
and burning the 1,000 businesses, destroying
homes worth millions. When the National Guard
arrives, it arrests the Black victims.

20 Min. Till the Polls Close
The Showdown
(Election Day 1972)

8 — INT. FARMHOUSE KITCHEN — NIGHT

Everyone is still seated around the kitchen table, 9-Yr-Old Faith in the midst of it all. Now that things have taken a serious turn, the Voice/Over is Grown-up Faith.

> **FAITH (VOICE/OVER)**
> After dinner, while my mother serves the pie (orange sherbet and vanilla ice milk in a checkerboard pattern for me), Mummi Lempi is already up at the sink, washing plates, arranging the leftovers in lidded glass boxes, wiping the stove and counter tops. While we finish our desserts, she slices last night's roast chicken and gets a sandwich assembly line going for tomorrow's lunches. She adds pie wedges wrapped in wax paper and pale Golden Delicious apples from the orchard down the road and thermoses of milk or coffee. She latches the boxes shut and puts a pie

tin of venison and chicken scraps in the
laundry room to take to the barn cats.

MUMMI LEMPI
(sings out)
Almost ready.

Mummi wipes her hands on her apron and heads down the hall.
When she reappears, changed into heels and hose, Mom looks up
from *Time* magazine and shakes her head.

MOM
You can take the girl out of the city.

FAITH (VOICE/OVER)
Mummi Lempi wraps her wool coat with
the "ERA Now" button on the lapel
around her, and we hop into the yellow
Chevy. Morfar Gib and Uncle Michael-
Väinö will take the blue pickup and meet
us at the polls. It's just a mile to town,
where we'll swing by Täti Rauha's house
and lean on the horn until she ditches
whichever Republican she's married to at
present and scurries out in a cloud of face
powder and Coty's Emeraude (a smell like
her big pink bottle of rose lotion and Uncle
Michael-Väinö's incense sticks and Mummi
Lempi's vanilla extract had a baby).

9 — INT. MUMMI'S CAR—NIGHT

Mummi and Mom in the front, Faith in the backseat, beneath a scratchy Pendleton wool car blanket. She presses her face to the window as they glide past asparagus fields and barbed wire fences, Mom and Mummi Lempi conferring in low, urgent tones.

MUMMI LEMPI

It is ON-ly TWEN-ty-three LIT-tle words—

E-qual rights RE-gardless of sex! I CAN-not BE-lieve ve haf been FIGHT-ing for this since SUF-frage!

MOM

Well, the time has finally come. ERA sailed through the House and Senate, and nearly a third of the states have ratified it.

MUMMI LEMPI

(shuddering)

Yeah, but this PHYL-lis SCHLAF-ly and her STOP ERA FOLLowers are VER-y loud.

MOM

(hands waving)

Unbelievable! How can any woman In Her Right Mind not want equal rights under the law? Even Slimy Nixon supports it! Her followers are just like the idiot housewives in that book I got from the library, *The Stepford Wives*.

MUMMI LEMPI

(skeptical)

The one by the AU-thor of ROSE-mary's BA-by?

MOM

Yeah, but you know I don't do horror. This is kinda thriller, kinda satire, and well, kinda trashy. You should read it.

MUMMI LEMPI.

RE-gardless of vhat you think of your FAH-der, I am not OP-pressed HOUSE-wife.

9-YR-OLD FAITH

(head popping over the backseat)

Can I read it?

MOM

(turning and poking my nose lightly)

Nine is a little young, punkin. Maybe wait a few years.

MUMMI LEMPI

(taking the opportunity to change the topic)

SCHLAF-ly is TELL-ing PE-E-ple that an Equal Rights AH-mend-ment will be the end of NOR-mal life. VO-men will have to go fight in VI-et-nam, and HO-mosexuals vill DE-stroy AH-merican FAM-ilies.

MOM

Oh Lord.

MUMMI LEMPI

(lowers voice)

You know, your TÄ-ti A-lice was a bit FUN-ny.

9-YR-OLD FAITH
Funny? Did she make jokes like Morfar Gib?

I don't remember that.

MUMMI LEMPI
(lobs over her shoulder)
I don't think you EV-er met her, SWEET-ie.

(whispers to Mom)
I mean, she was that way.

MOM
(arches eyebrows)
Oh *real*-ly? Dad's favorite sister?

FAITH (VOICE/OVER)
Mom sounds impressed, and I imagine that
she's trying to reconcile Morfar Gib the
Queer Ally with what she's been calling
him all these years—Archie Bunker and
Bigot. Though no one could ever accuse
him of not supporting ERA or of being a
Male Chauvinist Pig like
Uncle Michael-Väinö.

10 — EXT. JR HIGH / POLLS PARKING LOT–NIGHT

Wide-angle shot of matte-purple softly undulating hills. Bandits appear on horseback on the horizon and ride across the screen, right to left, a dead giveaway that they are Bad Guys. They gather on the ridge, menacing. A high-angle shot from behind looks down on to the village.

> **FAITH (VOICE/OVER)**
> From the back window of Mummi Lempi's pale yellow Chevy, I watch the women in my family assemble ominously on Main Street (a.k.a., the Junior High School parking lot). They knot wool scarves backwards over hairdos spun light as cotton candy, adjust shimmering hose,

smooth leather driving gloves over fingers
in slow, determined strokes that mean
business. Eying each other up like the
gunmen in *The Magnificent Seven*, each
gives a quick, sober nod. Mom leans down,
flips forward the heavy vinyl seat and
crooks her chin at me.

MOM

C'mon, kid.

FAITH (VOICE/OVER)

I scramble out. Clearly, voting is serious
business.

Mummi, Täti, Mom, and 9-Yr-Old Faith walk side-by-side through
the rows of cars toward the Junior High School. Suddenly, out from
behind a parked Chevy Camaro (muscle car of choice among Uncle
Michael-Väinö's crew) steps Grown-up Faith. She watches her family
and her child-self pass by, then falls into step behind them, undetected.

FAITH

(talks over her shoulder to the camera)
In another twenty years, life will imitate art. In
the original *Magnificent Seven* (1960), after bandits
terrorize a village of Mexican peasant farmers,
three villagers cross into Texas in search of
gunslingers to help defend them. It's a Western-
Western remake of *Seven Samurai (*1954), an
Eastern-Western about seven rōnin (masterless
samurai) who protect a farming village during
Japan's warring states period.

In time, the landscape of my childhood—orchards of gnarled apple and cherry trees, beaded hop and grape vines, asparagus fields calling for cheap labor—will eventually transform into a Mexican American village. Its migrant farmworkers will also need protection. Just like the Japanese American farmers who proceeded them and had their lands seized during World War II. And the native peoples, the Yakama, before them.

But even now, among the white descendants of German Baptist migrants from the south and Dust Bowl refugees and European immigrants like us, the stakes are high.

The women in my family swagger in a pack across the parking lot, pocketbooks dangling from raglan sleeves. From the set of their jaws, the glitter in their Nordic-blue eyes, it's evident they're prepared to do whatever it takes to defend this town from The Republicans.

Half way to the building we are joined by our men.

Morfar Gib and Uncle Michael-Väinö join the line-up, walking side-by-side with Mummi, Täti, Mom and 9-Yr-Old Faith. (With invisible Grown-up Faith, they are now The Seven.)

Movie posters for Seven Samurai (1954), The Magnificent Seven (1960), &
The Magnificent Seven (2016)

FAITH (CONT'D)

(still over the shoulder to the camera)

Our family is obsessed with championing the
underdog. Morfar Gib is downright apoplectic
about the need to unionize workers and Bring
Our Boys Home. Mom has a library for every
situation—women who need Women's Lib,
countries in Africa, Asia and South America that
need to be free again—and sends money each
month to children without families and protesters
saying no to nuclear energy and animals without
homes. Mummi Lempi whispers support for
poor, shy immigrants and The Vote. And I—

(points to 9-Yr.-Old Faith)

—patrol the elementary school playground, on
the lookout for white teachers saying mean things
to Mexican and Chicano students and farm-boy

jocks torturing animals. (Until I hit puberty, no longer a cute kid, and everything changes, the white teachers and farm-boy jocks saying mean things and torturing me. It's hard to champion myself.)

BTW: The soundtrack to all this championing is the SCRITCH-SCRATCH of furious after-dinner letters to the editor, Joan Baez and Buffy Saint Marie wailing on the stereo console, with breaks for our family's favorite—movies, movies, movies. So back to:

"The Family as Magnificent Seven Gunslingers:"
*(gestures to family members in the parking
lot as she talks)*

MOM: Definitely The Leader. One, because she's the boss of me and probably Mummi too. Two, because she has it bad for likes-to-claim-he's-Mongolian-or-Romani-or-Tartar and dresses-all-in-black star Yul Brynner, who leads The Seven. Hollywood's original bald sexy man. A multiethnic Russian whose family lost their wealth during the Revolution (when the Red Army nationalized their property and didn't notice Finland sneaking out the back door), Yul is a racial shapeshifter. Over his career, he plays the following:

A problematic Thai king
A red-booted Cossack
An Egyptian pharaoh

An Arab revolutionary
A Mexican revolutionary
An Indian revolutionary
A Native American chief captured by Mayans
A half-Japanese, half-Polish Air Force sergeant
A king of Israel
A (magnificent!) American cowboy.

Mom also has it bad for Sidney "Looks-Just-Like-Your-Poppie" Poitier, suggesting that she may suffer in fact from Jungle Fever.

<u>MORFAR GIB</u>: Definitely The Hothead. One, because the gunslinger is portrayed by actor Horst Buchholz (the so-called "German James Dean") and when he was young, Morfar Gib looked like a Swedish Paul Newman, so, Europe. Two, because, well, hothead. Suffers from Must Get His Way-ism.

<u>UNCLE MICHAEL-VÄINÖ</u>:
Also a hothead, especially when he and his friends go out drinking, but most likely The Gambler. Because one, he too is a bit of a drifter and a gambler. And two, the gunslinger is played by tow-headed Steve McQueen, "The King of Cool" whom Uncle Michael-Väinö resembles and claims to have met once in the town dive bar.

<u>9-YR.-OLD FAITH</u>: Me. The Nice One. Not because I am particularly, but because like me the nice character Bernardo O'Reilly is biracial ("Irish on one side, Mexican on the other, and

me in the middle"), and because the 2016 remake starring Denzel Washington as The Leader (a Japanese rōnin turned fake-Asian cowboy turned Black American cowboy) is years away. Suffers from Can't Keep a Family Secret-ism.

MUMMI: Actually The Nice One, because O'Reilly is kind to children and notices the villagers' meager food supply used to pay the Seven. And because we are pretty much doubles. Suffers from Putting Up with the Rest of Us.

TÄTI RAUHA: We're never sure which character she'll be. Waspish great-aunt, Dime Store clerk, three-time wife. The one left in charge of Mummi and their brother when their mother went to work & work & work, and their father disappeared. Suffers from Nastiness, no, Nerves, no, Nastiness.

Whenever I trot my pony Bandit (Bandit!) around the back pasture, replaying the opening credits in my head, I mull over which of *The Magnificent Seven* Täti Rauha should be.

First, I think The Fortune Hunter—the role originated by Brad Dexter (a dimwit who in real life saved that Chauvinist Pig Frank Sinatra from drowning)—because Täti Rauha likes money. Then, I think maay-beee The Assassin, played by James Coburn, all coiled and deadly, because her barbs are as fast as knives ("It'llbeafineday!"), almost like she can't help herself.

As the family approaches the building, Grown-up Faith has gradually been lowering her voice, which finally returns to Voice/Over, though she remains with her family in the scene.

> **FAITH (VOICE/OVER)**
> My family fans out, swaggering toward the showdown. CLICK-CLICK-CLICK, handbags snap open and shut, pink voting cards lock into place.
>
> At last, we stride through the swinging doors to the Junior High School auditorium and stand shoulder-to-shoulder, surveying this rotten gang of union-busting ranchers and farmers.

11 — INT. JR HIGH SCHOOL GYM — NIGHT

Every townsperson inside whips aside their voting booth curtains and turns to stare. Suddenly we see the family from their POV: The Immigrants: Mummi, Täti Rauha, Morfar Gib. The Americans: Uncle Michael-Väinö and Mom. The Brown One: 9-Yr-Old Faith (Grown-up Faith has gone invisible). The double doors of the Junior High School slowly click shut behind them.

The action FREEZES.

FAITH (VOICE/OVER)
How did we end up voting here, in
this movie, this town? First my Nordic
immigrant grandparents, then my white
American mom and uncle, finally, mixed-
race me? In this dry thumbprint of earth
cupped in a ring of sagebrush hills so matte
and purple they could have been a painted
backdrop for one of the Westerns Mom and
Uncle Michael-Väinö grew up on (different
double feature every weekend, yee-haw!).

This is perhaps how:

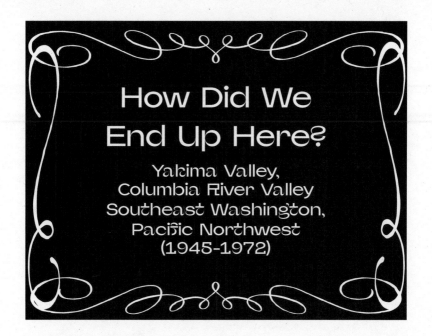

How Did We
End Up Here?

Yakima Valley,
Columbia River Valley
Southeast Washington,
Pacific Northwest
(1945-1972)

12 — EXT. YAKIMA VALLEY — DAY

Scene opens to a pristine valley. As the Voice/Over begins to describe the land's evolution, two pairs of Yakama natives in full ceremonial regalia appear on horseback, riding double. They halt, and two women dismount and stand between the horses. All four, plus their horses, stand with their backs to the camera, peering out over the soon-to-be-invaded valley.

> **FAITH (VOICE/OVER)**
> First the Finns and Swedes, dreaming of
> America, left their villages, took a train,
> crossed an ocean, sat in quarantine on the
> tip of the New World, and took another
> series of trains West. At the end of the line
> sat a wet emerald-green city of trees not
> unlike the lumber towns they'd left behind,

in a new territory populated with indigenous
people not unlike the Sami they'd left behind
(who were eventually pushed onto state
reserves), with laborers imported from China
(before the Exclusion Act), with Filipino and
Japanese farmers (denied citizenship and later
incarcerated during World War II), with brown
vaqueros and black cowboys (who retired into
rural or urban poverty respectively), with
white male settlers and their women, who kept
winning and losing the vote until 1920, when
the 19th Amendment made female suffrage
federal law—for white women.

Papers filed, America achieved, the
immigrants moved inland in search of
farmland and came to a stop when they
saw scrub hills and a big blue bowl of
sky. Millions of acres stretching across
Washington's central plateau, up along
the Rattlesnake Hills, a spine of grasses
and tumbleweeds, down along the blond
scrub and striated vistas of the Horse
Heaven Hills, over to the Columbia River
carving 1,250 miles of border from British
Columbia to Oregon's Pacific Ocean.

TIME LAPSE footage of the Yakama Valley begins: The land
changing before our eyes, filling up with barns, businesses, marquee
lights. Finnish siblings drift through on a couch, looking into the
camera, followed by Baby Faith and her black-and-white sheepdog,
Lady. Dressed as tiny, misguided cowboys, young Uncle Mike and two
cousins cluster together behind the Yakama, who stand motionless
and disapproving with their backs to us.

FAITH (VOICE/OVER
The immigrants plowed farms and towns
onto land belonging to the Yakama Nation
of Confederated Tribes & Bands, who
(despite the Act of 1924 granting Native
Americans U.S. citizenship and despite the
15th Amendment granting "all citizens,"
i.e., men, the vote) wouldn't really get the
vote until Civil Rights legislation in 1965.
With the rest of us.

Unions joined, middle-classdom achieved,
my grandparents drove to town and
deposited their American kids, fists
clutching shiny coins, at the movie parlor.
Sunday-stiff in their new dungarees and
cowboy boots, red felt bolero hats dangling
from strings around their necks, Mom
and Uncle Michael-Väinö rushed inside to
cheer white cowboys.

Eventually Mom stopped cheering
and tried to leave. Repeatedly. But our
permanent, father-less return to small-
town Washington when I am six seems
inevitable. We're the human equivalent
of salmon, after all, bound to come back
to birth and to die. (If only small daily
deaths.) Yet, to the end we'll persevere, and
we'll resist, just like Mummi did for Mom,
and Mom did for me.

The Leaders of the Seven: Toshiro Mifune (1954), Yul Brynner (1960),
Denzel Washington (2016), Mummi, and Mom.

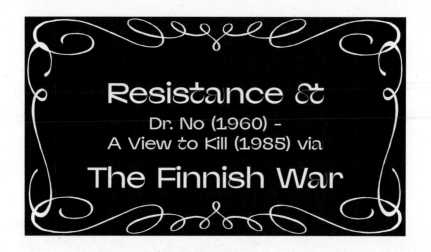

Resistance &
Dr. No (1960) –
A View to Kill (1985) via
The Finnish War

13 — EXT. DRAMATIC SKI SLOPES IN ICELAND

College-Age Faith traverses the slopes wearing a white linen dress with detachable shoulder sashes crisscrossing her chest. She pauses frequently at breathtaking overlooks to talk. As she combines scenes with images from memories, they're projected onto the snowy mountainside as if onto a movie screen. James Bond reports for duty to Finnish ski troopers, who give him the side-eye. Baby Faith ducks the paparazzi, accompanied by Lady the Sheepdog, who ogles the Finnish reindeer corps. Grace Jones steps off an album cover and flexes, glistening and underdressed.

COLLEGE-AGE FAITH
(almost shouts to be heard over the sound of
her swooshing skis)
According to Mummi Lempi, the most exciting part of the Finnish resistance in the Winter War were the Ski Troopers, who wore all-white arctic camouflage with fur hoods ("and SOME-times a cape!"). Though we oppose the Vietnam War, the Talvisota is a war everyone can get behind. It has

fashion, Evil Russians oppressing Stoic Finns (the ultimate underdogs!) yet again, and eventually even receives an homage from James Bond. In our family, Double-O-Seven is a biannual event that has the men checking the newspaper, buzzing with anticipation like schoolboys, and roaring to the Starlight Drive-in opening night.

At college, after Mummi and Morfar have died and Uncle Michael-Väinö has started to rewrite history (a narrative that doesn't include us), I attend a late-night screening of *Dr. No*, the first-ever James Bond film. The lush Kingston and Ocho Rios locations provide the perfect escape from finals, and Sean-Connery Bond is way cooler than the Roger-Moore Bond of my childhood. Even better, a camaraderie develops between Bond and Quarrel, a knowledgeable Cayman Islander portrayed by American actor John Kitzmiller (who was huge in Europe). The two men race across Jamaica's beaches doing interracial spy-buddy things until Swiss actress Ursula Andress emerges from the sea in a white bikini, blonde tresses wet and glistening, the cinematic equivalent of breaking the internet.

Bond promptly strong-arms her into joining their merry band and soon barks at Quarrel, "Fetch my shoes!"

The entire college audience shouts astonished disapproval, which makes it hurt just a little less. But Quarrel does indeed fetch, and for 26 seconds I'm forced to watch him run after the golden couple, carrying Bond's loafers in his mahogany hands.

Cut to robotic supervillain Dr. No of the shiny black mechanical hands, who refers to himself as the "unwanted child of a German missionary and a Chinese girl of a good family."

In the darkened dining-hall-turned-screening-room, my stomach starts to knot again. Not only is the maniacal villain a biracial bastard (literally), but the actor portraying him is obviously white.

This, I've just learned in my film studies class, is called Yellowface, analog to the Blackface with which I am already familiar. Connery trains his liquid brown eyes on the camera and snipes, "With your disregard for human life, you must be working for the East." We hoot with derision, and come school break, I've recovered enough to watch *A View to a Kill,* Moore's final turn as Bond.

As the pre-titles roll, my mouth unhinges at the sight of Bond in a white jumpsuit with fur-lined hood, white gloves, white skis, white backpack, and white-frame aviator sunglasses. I tap Mom and lean forward, staring hard as a helicopter crests the hill. Cut to the soldiers below, who head up the mountain on skis and snowmobiles, shouting in Russian. Now I'm sure; this is supposed to be Siberia, and Moore's designer Bogden suit (which he can't really carry off in his late-fifties) is clearly inspired by Finnish ski troopers.

The rest of the nearly ten-minute sequence is all downhill racing, schussing down headwalls, as ski patrols pursue him with machine guns, and the helicopter with the red star on the side twists above. Eventually Bond hops into a submarine "disguised" as an iceberg that looks like a high school drama prop and unpacks a tin of Beluga caviar, a bottle of Stoly vodka, and a microchip.

The female agent piloting the sub has a breathy voice, plunging neckline, and Farrah Fawcett-style frosted hair. I hear Mom hiss, but I'm so excited at the nod to Finnish resistance that I'm prepared to overlook Rapey Bond. "Be a good girl, would you," he orders, grabbing her, "and put her on automatic. We could do with a couple of glasses."

Generations of 007: Sean Connery's first and Roger Moore's last

The Family as James Bond Characters, Heroes? / Villains?

College-Age Faith skids to an elegant stop on the mountain slope. Panting, she side-steps up to a free-standing whiteboard placed conveniently next to a pine tree.

> **COLLEGE-AGE FAITH — CONT'D**
> *(writes on the whiteboard as she speaks)*
> UNCLE MICHAEL-VÄINO: Bond himself.
> Because he clearly idolizes the fictional MI6
> agent, played by Sean Connery when Uncle
> Michael-Väinö is watching in his 20s, Roger
> Moore in his 30s, Moore and Timothy Dalton
> in his 40s. Suffers from an Unnamed Handicap
> (shhh!) and (like all 007s) drinking, smoking,
> gambling, sexism and quasi-racism.
>
> ME (COLLEGE-AGE FAITH): May Day.
> Because in college I'm obsessed with the
> supervillain's superhuman henchwoman. May
> Day is played to sleek, snarly perfection by
> androgynous Jamaican model/performer/
> actress Grace Jones. (Later that year I will
> be captivated by her concept album *Slave to
> the Rhythm*, its dance tracks interspersed with
> commentary about her life and recitations
> from *Jungle Fever*, the biography of her
> ex-partner Jean-Paul Goude, designer of Jones'

iconic, anatomically-impossible Island Life pose and lover of Blackwomen and Blackface everywhere.) Suffers from Exotic Erotic casting.

MORFAR GIB: KGB agent Venz. Because he's played by a Swedish chemical-engineer-turned-body-guard-turned-actor. And Morfar Gib is a Swedish-American naval-officer-turned-photojournalist-turned-construction foreman who can build anything. In real life, Dolph Lundgren is Grace Jones' boyfriend, which makes it a little weird. Later that year Lundgren's real breakthrough will come when he portrays a superhuman Soviet boxer in *Rocky IV*, essentially the white-blond exotic equivalent of blue-black May Day.

THE SUPERVILLAIN: There are too many supervillains around us to count. There's the Religious Right who founded this town and regularly tells us we're going to hell. There are Union Busters and War Hawks. There are Bigots, which are what you call racists and classists and misogynists and homophobes when you live in a village and are outnumbered and outgunned, the cowboys as scary as the bandits. Real villains aren't as smart or deliciously wicked as Christopher Walken playing Bond's nemesis, Max Zorin. Product of a Nazi (of course!) genetic experiment, Zorin plans to detonate explosives beneath the Hayward and San Andreas Faults, sink Silicon Valley, and seize control of the microchip

market. Suffers from psychopathy and (like all
007 supervillains) overly elaborate evil planning.

14 — INT. SMALL TOWN COURTHOUSE—DAY

FLASHBACK to a memory of village villainry. Mummi Lempi
and 7-Yr-Old Faith stand in line at the courthouse, speaking in low
voices. A languid clerk behind glass chats with a colleague, his back
to the customers waiting in line. As College-Age Faith describes her
memory of the event, we watch the scene unfold. . .

> **COLLEGE-AGE FAITH (VOICE/OVER)**
> Because drinking, smoking, gambling,
> sexism, and quasi-racism pay off better
> when you're actually James Bond, there's
> no voting for our twenty-four-year-old,
> delinquent, Bond-wannabe Uncle Michael-
> Väinö. But Mummi Lempi is here to make
> things right for his future. . . .
> That's what women do.

> We were already here at the courthouse
> earlier this morning to find out the rules,
> and then we left to wait in line at Old
> National Bank to withdraw the money
> for the fees. Now we're back again, Uncle
> Mike's petition (filled out by Mummi
> Lempi) in hand (hers). The courthouse
> is all polished wood and gray metal
> file cabinets. I sniff, trying to place the
> chemicals. We stand arms akimbo, all

Magnificent Seven like, squinted eyes
giving nothing away.

Though it's Morfar Gib and Mom shouting
politics during dinner and scribbling letters
to the ombudsman over dessert, Mummi
Lempi defends the Free World too. Finnish
women were the first in the Western world
to win national suffrage

MUMMI LEMPI
(speaks one audible line to 7-Yr-Old Faith)
. . . NEAR-ly a DE-cade and a half BE-fore A-merica!

COLLEGE-AGE FAITH (VOICE/OVER)
Whenever possible, Mummi Lempi and
Täti Rauha (wo)man the polls. Imagine,
two immigrant ex-waitresses safeguarding
the most powerful right of citizens of the
most powerful country in the world!

CLERK
(In a loud, bored voice)
Next!

COLLEGE-AGE FAITH (VOICE/OVER)
Mummi Lempi grips my hand, and I
glance up, surprised. She is trembling as we
approach the counter. Over a decade later, I
can still feel her warm flesh on mine,
still quivering.

MUMMI LEMPI
(Whispering)
GUD AFT-ernoon. I vould like to file this BE-tition to have my
son's YU-venile RE-cord sealed.

CLERK
(In mocking singsong)
Huh? His yoo-vuh-what?

COLLEGE-AGE FAITH (VOICE/OVER)
Mummi Lempi wilts—perhaps she is really
tortured Robert Vaughn, brave and yet
terrified he's a coward—and I want to
shout, "Juvenile! She said 'juvenile', you
ignoramus!" But two wrongs don't
make a right.

The clerk notices me, dark-hearted and
cinnamon-faced, below the counter
and stares open-mouthed from Mummi
Lempi to me, back to Mummi Lempi. I'm
torn between my twin powers: charm or
battle? Though Mummi Lempi can shoot
a gun, dropping the venison she stews
for us, Mom has seen to it that I've never
even held one. Instead, my eyes narrow,
willing a giant magnifying glass above
the courthouse. With our weather (360
days of sun, according to the Chamber of
Commerce), it's only a matter of minutes
before the clerk's head explodes into flame.
It'll be a fine day.

MUMMI LEMPI
(quavering voice)
I HAF the fee.

COLLEGE-AGE FAITH (VOICE/OVER)
She hoists her voluminous handbag onto
the counter and rifles inside for the bank
envelope. I squint, angling the giant
magnifying glass. *Faster-faster-faster.* The
clerk squints back, *squinch-squinch-squinch,*
oblivious to his near-death.

MUMMI LEMPI
(pulls her hand out of her bag and blinks)
Oh my!

COLLEGE-AGE FAITH (VOICE/OVER)
She stands in the middle of the courthouse,
all red lipstick and navy pumps and
sapphire rhinestones, in one hand a bank
envelope of cash, in the other a paper towel
nest of bacon.

Almost-incinerated clerk forgotten, we each
internally race to reconstruct
the chain of events:

15 — EXT. FARMHOUSE / INT. CAR - (EARLIER)

Quick FLASHBACK (memory) of Mummi Lempi heading towards
the barn with scraps for the cats; Mom bursting out the backdoor,
late for work; the jump into the car, ANGLE ON bacon atop the
handbag's open maw.

> FAITH (VOICE/OVER)
> Mummi Lempi will save the Free World, and
> Uncle Michael-Väinö will vote again.

> MOM (VOICE/OVER)
> *(snorting)*
> Hmph, God knows for whom!

> FAITH (VOICE/OVER)
> Mommm! *I* do the VOICE/OVER!

16 — INT. SMALL TOWN COURTHOUSE

Quick FLASHBACK ENDS: Clerk, Mummi, and Faith, dumbstruck over found bacon.

> FAITH (VOICE/OVER)
> But for us the punchline is always Mummi
> Lempi's bemused response to the clerk.

> MUMMI LEMPI
> But the last time ve had BA-con vas a veek A-go!

17 — EXT. DRAMATIC SKI SLOPES IN ICELAND

College-age Faith, still standing at the whiteboard on the mountainside.

> COLLEGE-AGE FAITH
> *(jots down notes as she "lectures")*

What's Black & White
& Red All Over?

In 1919, after the Great War and the Russian
Revolution, Americans simply can't figure out
which of its tired, its poor, its huddled masses
yearning to breathe free to despise more.

The striking steel workers?
The striking coal miners?
The striking longshoremen?
The striking railroad workers?
The striking Boston policemen?
The 100-plus local unions participating in the
Seattle General Strike?

It's tough, as an estimated one-fifth of all U.S.
workers strike that year. Perhaps members of
the newly-founded American Communist Party,
those emboldened Bolsheviks? The anarchists
actually setting off bombs? Or that old standby,
tried-and-true—Black communities finally
making economic headway?

College-Age Faith, abruptly sets off down the mountain, kicking
sprays of powder at the camera lens until . . .

7 Seconds Later
(9 Min. & 53 Seconds Till the Polls Close)
The Magnificent Seven (2016) **- Redo**

18 — INT. JR HIGH SCHOOL AUDITORIUM

Still standing (frozen in time) side-by-side just inside the doors of the Junior High School auditorium, like seven magnificent gunslingers or samurai, Grown-up Faith and her family of six return to action, milling about. 9-Yr-Old Faith, aghast that only 7 seconds have passed under the scrutiny of the townspeople, looks to her grown-up self, as if catching glimpses of a braver future.

FAITH
(recognizes the look and joins her 9-Yr-Old self)
Though I'm fully adult by the time *The Magnificent Seven* is remade for the big screen and have no horse in that race, a Western with politics (that don't make me cringe) is a portal back to childhood.

Besides, Denzel dipping his toe into a new genre demands our support!

Three generations of magnificent gunslingers

It's been four decades after all since Sidney "Looks Just Like [My] Poppie" Poitier directed and starred in *Buck and the Preacher*. Perhaps the first Western to center Black actors, portray Black and Native American relations, and show Black folks fighting back against whites. I have high hopes. Unfortunately, there are two essential flaws.

First is: Though the gunslingers are finally appropriately international and multiracial, the village of Mexican peasants they're contracted to save has been transformed into white settlers. I pause my laptop and Google the director. Yes, a Black man has assembled an authentic cast that's nonetheless going to get him accused of political correctness, even historical revision, and then inexplicably given them the mission of protecting white innocence.

It's a bit like watching *Birth of a Nation* updated with settler-colonizers and Manifest Destiny. Particularly when Red Harvest, a Comanche warrior sporting stunning red, black, and white face paint, leaps in front of the Bad Indian advancing menacingly toward a white woman, who up until now has been a bad-ass part of the gunslingers. By way of backstory, Red Harvest, portrayed by an actual native actor (albeit Athabaskan-Tlingit from Alaska), says he's a loner then rips out a deer's kidney and takes a raw bloody bite. I feel a bit like that deer. Before killing and throwing his tribesmen off a balcony, he whispers to him in Comanche, "You're a disgrace."

Second is: What now drives bounty-hunter Denzel is *personal* revenge, which (though a familiar trope in the American loner arsenal) is hardly Magnificent. The whole point of *The Magnificent Seven* (and even more so *Seven Samurai,* who were paid only in food and the opportunity to regain their honor) is a Pyrrhic victory, a noble, devastating sacrifice for a greater good. In Finnish we call it sisu, stoic grit in the face of the impossible, and the whole world saw it during the Winter War, when volunteers on skis with rifles and reindeer took on Soviet tanks. Seven ride in, three ride out.

EVERY NARRATOR (VOICE/OVER)
(as if sounding through the school P.A. system)
> They fought for the ones who couldn't fight for themselves. And they died for them too. All to win what didn't belong to them. It was magnificent.

FAITH
Instead of a supposedly-Mexican bandit king (Eli Wallach in Brownface), the supervillain in the remake of the remake is an evil industrialist played by Peter Sarsgaard (like us, Nordic-American, but that's small consolation).
(suddenly spotting a long-forgotten minor character across the room)
Blanche, our inside man at the polls, her shock of pure white hair cut like a boy's, shouts at us.

BLANCHE
Hey, Kid! You made it!

9-Yr-Old-Faith heads straight toward Blanche, gesturing to her milling family members, now in danger of being too late to vote.

9-YR-OLD FAITH

*(speaks to the camera? to her invisible
grown-up self keeping up behind her?)*
Blanche lives directly across the street from Täti Rauha and calls everyone "kid". She and two other 60-year-old kids sit at a folding table checking pink cards. The auditorium is bright and decorated as if for the dances to which I won't be invited, but in red, white, and blue.

FAITH

My people belly up to the table in clicking heels and flash their voting cards. Blanche taps a thick finger on a clipboard.

BLANCHE

Sign here, Kid. *Kid. Kid.* You got just 7 minutes till the polls close.

FAITH

They all grunt and split up, disappearing into separate curtained booths that resemble portable camp showers with a metal Hula Hoop on top holding a curtain on rings—

9-YR-OLD FAITH

—but where the hot- and cold-water handles should be are banks of little windows with important choices written in them and small dark

levers like in a fuse box. At the bottom is a large
lever to close the curtain.

FAITH
I wait in a folding chair next to Blanche and ask
again about her cat, rumored to be eighteen years
old.

9-Yr-Old-Faith sits in the chair as Blanche leans toward her
conspiratorially.

FAITH (CONT)
Whenever Täti Rauha and I are outside
gardening, Blanche and her husband Tommy the
Plumber will wave ("Hey Kid!") and call me over
to their pristine lawn, forest green against the
pale-mint house and velvety crimson rose bushes.

Begin FLASHBACK:

19—EXT. TÄTI RAUHA'S SMALL RED HOUSE — DAY

Täti Rauha wanders the front yard with a garden hose, wearing
glamorous pink Capri pants. 7-Yr-Old Faith, brown knees scuffed
below yellow shorts, crouches on the front stoop watching her.

BLANCHE
(shouts from her yard)
Hey Kid!

7-Yr-Old Faith and Blanche lounge together gossiping and laughing
while Tommy hovers nearby.

FAITH (VOICE/OVER)

Whenever Blanche and I recline on their
fancy chaises with tumblers of homemade
lemonade, she shouts with laughter and
tells me Sunnyside history: How her people
were Basque sheepherders who ran herds
along the scrublands up north, just like
back in the Old Country. How Old Doc
Querin, the large-animal vet, turned out
to be a Real-Life Bigamist, a whole second
family stashed away in the next town! And
how when the poor first wife . . .

BLANCHE

(interupts Faith as she yells to Tommy)
—a real looker, like Sophia Loren—right,
Tommy?

FAITH (VOICE/OVER)

. . . how when Doc Querin's first wife
found out, she returned to Italy,
leaving him their two boys, as well as
"the third secret child . . ."

20 — INT. MOM'S MOBILE HOME KITCHEN — NEXT DAY

Still in FLASHBACK, the day after 7-Yr-Old Faith and Blanche's
gossip session. The small kitchen of a single-wide mobile home. The
walls are dark faux-wood paneling; the linoleum is faux-pebbles-in-
a-stream; the appliances are avocado green. Holly and young Faith

sit at the small breakfast table, mid-discussion. Young Faith mid-statement . . .

7-YR-OLD FAITH
. . . A Mongoloid!

FAITH (VOICE/OVER)
(takes a beat)
. . . I announce brightly to Mom, parroting Blanche
and imagining perhaps a tiny Yul Brynner, a mini
remake, but Mom shakes her head angrily.

MOM
Faith! Don't ever let me hear you use that word
again!

FAITH (VOICE/OVER)
She doesn't tell me what to use, however, so it takes years
before I learn the medical term for this never-seen child
who's a secret for more than one reason. And it's years
before the Silver Screen West will come close to *our* West,
with its black cowboys and Mexican vaqueros, its Native
American warriors and trackers and fishermen, its Asian
farmers and laborers, its women who keep demanding
and winning and losing and demanding and winning
the right to vote.

YUL BRYNNER
BINGO

NAME THAT
ETHNIC GROUP

21 — INT. JR HIGH SCHOOL AUDITORIUM

FLASHBACK ends; we return to the Voting Polls where Grown-up Faith has found another whiteboard to write on:

Minor Characters

FAITH
*(mimicking College-Age Faith with a toss of
her tassled knit hat)*

<u>TOMMY & BLANCHE</u>: International man of mystery and butch daughter of Basque sheepherders. Tommy plays *The Gambler*— easygoing, stoic, fond of card tricks.

Favorite saying (Blanche): Hey kid!
Favorite saying (Tommy): Yup.

<u>DOC QUERIN</u>: Laconic vet who specializes in dairy cows and literal work horses. Bigamist who, along with his secret second wife, raises two sons (never a reference to the cursed third child), a red-head and a dark, good-natured, good-looking pothead. Once stormed out of surgery and screamed at Faith for bringing a stray to be spayed that turned out to be pregnant. "The operation killed the kittens!" he roared before bursting into sobs. Plays *The Gunslinger Who's Lost His Nerve*, portrayed in the remake by Ethan Hawke as a former Confederate sharpshooter suffering from PTSD. Favorite saying: Hmpf!

<u>TABBY CAT</u>: If rumors are true, 88 years old in human years. Plays the stray tabby on the studio lot that lucked into sitting on Marlon Brando's lap in *The Godfather* (1972) or Duchess, the cartoon

heiress cat in *The AristoCats* (1970), voiced by
Hungarian bombshell Zsa Zsa Gabor (Morfar
Gib's favorite). Favorite saying: Meow!

We see 9-Yr-Old Faith still waiting for the adults to finish voting.
She sits in the folding chair next to Blanche, legs swinging in those
Famolare shoes with the wavy crepe soles. Grown-up Faith returns to
her side again, studying her former self, remembering . . .

> **FAITH**
>
> I squirm and wonder about the mysterious
> adult things taking place behind the
> heavy curtains. Even though they think
> they're private, I can see everyone's legs.
> Mom taps her foot, legs bare in rope-soled
> espadrilles.

BLANCHE
*(following 9-Yr-Old Faith's eyes and
jerking her head at Mom's shoes)*
The Basque invented those.

> **FAITH**
>
> Mom's already read the Official Voters
> Pamphlet cover to cover, all 112 pages,
> studied the recommendations by the
> League of Women Voters and the National
> Organization for Women and the National
> Education Association and marked her
> answers in the practice test in front. She
> flicks the small switches in her booth
> quickly, *click-click-click*, then gives a little
> hoot, and I know she must have found

House Joint Resolution 61, the Proposed
Constitutional Amendment for
Sex Equality.

Mummi Lempi pivots slowly in glittery
hose and the navy pumps with the chunky
heel. She's taking her time, re-reading every
last word about things called Initiative
Measures and Referendum Bills, because we
need to regulate something called electoral
campaign financing, so that The Rich don't
become supervillains, and we need to collect
bonds to build more community colleges, so
that everyone can get an education and live
the American Dream.

Who knows what Täti Rauha in her white
kitten heels and a seam up the back of her
hose (like in old movies) is up to? Whenever
she says pulling the handle feels like playing
the slots in Reno, Mom looks pointedly at
me, and I know I'm supposed to disregard
that last comment, just like the jury on
Perry Mason (Mummi's favorite), because
we don't gamble, especially with our future.

One minute to go.
Then finally, I hear three metallic
thuds and rings as levers are pulled and
curtains sweep back. I hold my breath.

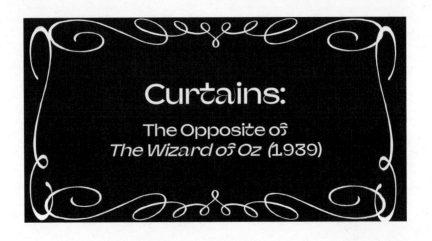

Curtains:

The Opposite of
The Wizard of Oz (1939)

It's the opposite of the moment in *The Wizard of Oz* when Toto gets the green curtain caught in his collar and reveals that the Great and Terrible Oz is merely a pink-faced man in a suit manipulating wheels and levers in a circular booth that looks just like these. Caught, he nonetheless turns his back to farmgirl Dorothy and announces into the intercom, "Pay no attention to that man behind the curtain!"

Mom says *The Wizard of Oz* is A Godawful Film. Whenever Some Fool in the faculty lounge or at one of Morfar's card parties starts arguing that it symbolizes the things we care about and tells her she should appreciate that the Scarecrow represents American farming and the Tin Man the U.S. steel industry and the Cowardly Lion her beloved Democrats (which doesn't really feel like a compliment), she crosses her eyes.

I have to try new things, even vegetables, but she already knows what she likes. When I say, that's "No fair," she says, "Fair enough," she'll try to be Less Judgmental. Just not about *The Wizard of Oz*.

When Mummi says that *The Wizard of Oz* helped Finnish moviegoers during the long, cold, hungry, decidedly-un-Technicolor years of war, Mom says Hmpf!

Finland went straight from the Winter War, where we were heroic underdogs against Russia, to the War of Continuation, our version of WWII, which is kinda embarrassing unless you believe that the enemy of your enemy (ie, Soviets) is your war ally (ie, Nazis).

The women in my family reemerge from behind their curtains, stronger than before, not easily fooled by bankers or politicians, pink cheeks flushed with success. Now it's time to go wait in front of the television for the rest of the country to tally our returns. Because every vote matters.

BLANCHE

Bye, Kid!

FAITH

We stride out, thumbs looped in belts, satisfied smiles.

Hrs. & Hrs. After

22 — INT. TÄTI RAUHA'S KITCHEN—NIGHT

Tati Rauha's house is fussy and fascinating in the way that people without kids can afford. As Faith narrates, we see the scenes she describes unfold.

> **FAITH (VOICE/OVER)**
> Moments later, we are back at Täti Rauha's place in town watching her reheat the morning's tea ("You can take the girl out of the Depression . . .") and excavate an assortment of gustamisses (that's Finnglish, which is like Spanglish, for anything sweet) inexplicably wrapped first in paper towel, then foil, then plastic wrap. Blocks of marzipan and fudge, slices of dry nissua (Mom's favorite), small town American cookies from "the girls" at work, with their strange mini-marshmallow and breakfast cereal fillings.

> We cluster around the dinette table, and I shovel nut-studded squares of fudge into my mouth while the women in my family grouse.

> **MOM**
> Can you believe eight Referendums, six Initiatives

and eight Joint Resolutions? I thought we'd be
there all night!

MUMMI LEMPI
ERA or no ERA, ven, will there be a FE-male PRES-ident?

FAITH (VOICE/OVER)
They whisper so that the current Republican husband
won't overhear from his television vigil in the living
room and start One of His Asinine Arguments.

1972 will be Mummi's last presidential election. During
the 1974 midterms, two months after Idiot Gerald Ford
grants Tricky Dick a full and unconditional pardon
for crimes committed, she will be battling cancer.

23 — INT. FARMHOUSE KITCHEN — NIGHT

FLASHBACK to Midterm Election Day 1970, two years before.
Mummi stands by the oven, peering through a tiny window in the
door at a pie. 7-Yr-Old Faith sits at the kitchen table, rearranging old
black-and-white family photographs in front of her. Behind her hangs
a calendar marked with red stars.

FAITH (VOICE/OVER)
Red Star Days (as opposed to the other color stars on the kitchen
calendar that Mummi Lempi uses to track if we're all "REG-u-lar") are
always like this, no matter how small or local the election. Every vote
counts. In the 1970 midterms, Washington is fixing to become the
first state to legalize abortion—three years before Roe v. Wade—by
referendum. A record number of voters turns out—nearly 72 percent.

Mummi with Mom and Uncle Michael-Väinö on the hill

Since Mom teaches at the junior high, she voted right after school. Morfar reports that his construction crew carpool stopped at the polls on the way home from work. Mummi's face falls. Michael-Väinö's application is still pending, so he won't be voting. Who's left? Täti Rauha calls after dinner to say she had to work late at the store. Mummi tells her she needs to finish washing dishes and packing lunches and mopping the kitchen and ironing the men's work clothes and mending my school socks and feeding the barn cats, then she'll drive into town.

"Just call my name," I hum, *"and I'll be there."*

Mummi glances up briefly and smiles. It's the hit song from my new *Jackson 5* album, which I'm dying to play on the stereo.

But Mom and Morfar are watching the returns in the living room and hollering.

Just before eight o'clock, she glances at the big kitchen clock over the sink and gives a guttural HUH like a samurai. It's late, the latest she's ever been. After snatching up her pocketbook, she pulls on her black-and-red plaid Pendleton wool car coat over her jeans (jeans!), ties a fringed scarf around her head, and rushes out the door to the polls. Sometimes it's The Seven, sometimes it's just one saving the free world.

Upon her return, Mummi staggers silently past the rest of us still hollering in the living room, and slips into the bedroom at the end of the house. There she kicks off her galoshes, peels off her car coat, driving gloves, and jeans (jeans!) and drops them onto the vanity table with the giant round mirror. She unfurls the fringed scarf in a single, fluid motion. As it flutters to the carpet, she draws back the Chenille bedspread and tumbles into bed, cheeks pink with victory, to dream.

FADE OUT.

THE END

Acknowledgments

This slim volume is part of an epic project that involved many years of traveling, finding family, writing, investigating and researching. I was assisted by many people along the way and would like to thank those I remember and apologize to those I've inadvertently omitted.

First and foremost, I owe thanks to my mother for loving books and movies and for encouraging me since childhood to be a writer brave enough to look history in the eye. And to my husband for understanding that I need to go away to beautiful places to write.

To my fairy godmother agents, Ayesha Pande and the late Lynn Franklin, both generous and patient. To my writing partner, Elmaz Abinader, and our writing group members Tara Dorabji and Susan Ito, for cheering me on and reading multiple drafts.

To Deesha Philyaw for inviting me to share the John Grisham House while editing the final draft. Residencies at Write On Door County (Wisconsin) and CourCommune (Voulx, France) also provided the time and space to envision these projects.

To Gabrielle Civil for introducing me to Texas Review Press and reconnecting me with Peter Carlisle, whose brilliant and tireless edits, both written and visual, were an author's dream; to J. Bruce and Peter for deciding to accept both manuscripts, and to the entire TRP team for taking such care with chapbooks.

Finally, I am thankful for my colleagues at California College of the Arts, my assistant Anna Alves for handling the stuff I hate so that I can do the stuff I love, and you, dear reader